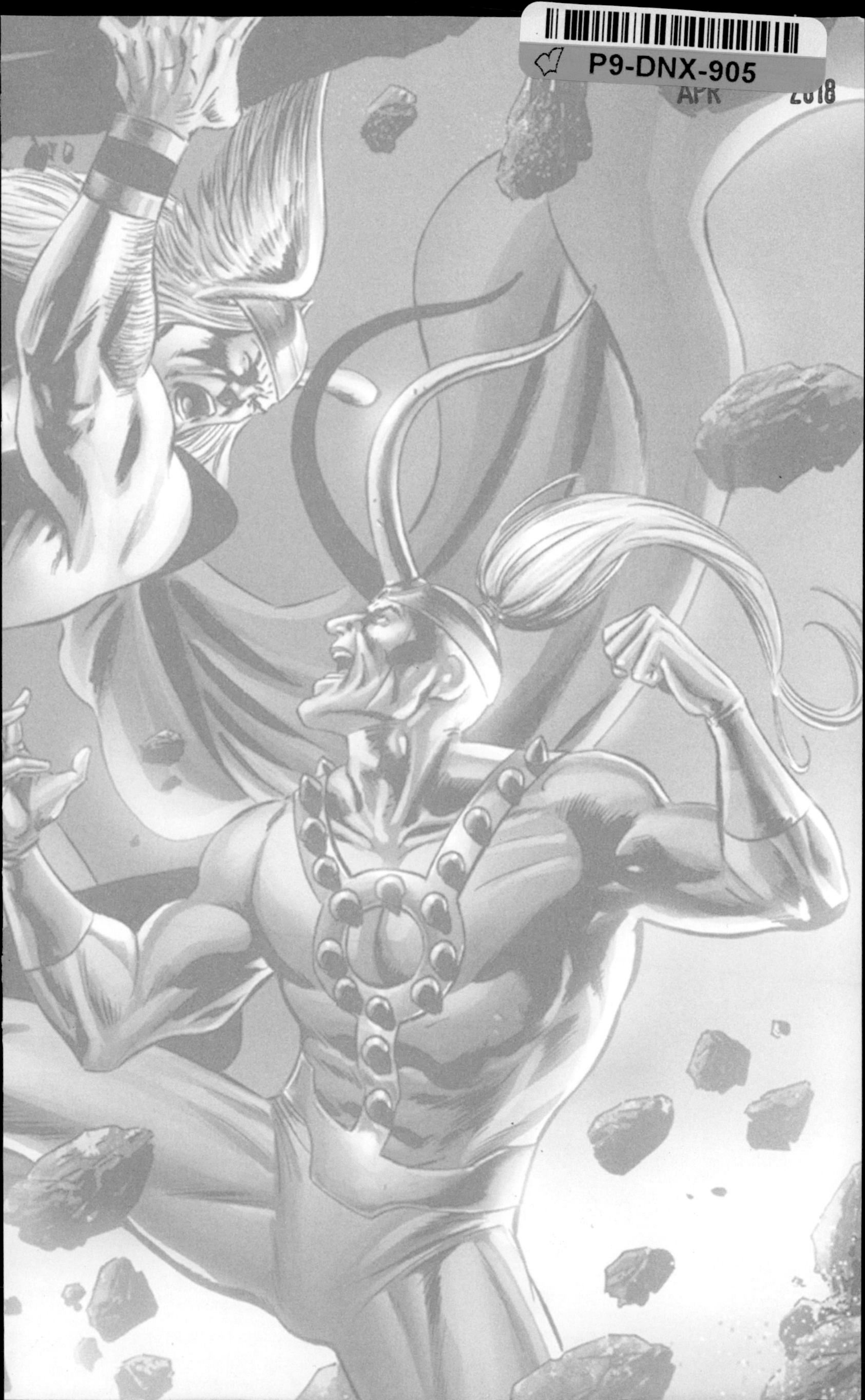

MARVEL

ULTIMATE VILLAINS

Written by Cefn Ridout

Editorial Assistant Natalie Edwards
Project Art Editor Jon Hall
Project Editor Ruth Amos
Pre-production Producer Marc Staples
Senior Producer Mary Slater
Managing Editor Sadie Smith
Managing Art Editor Vicky Short
Publisher Julie Ferris
Art Director Lisa Lanzarini
Publishing Director Simon Beecroft

Reading Consultant Linda B. Gambrell, Ph.D

First American Edition, 2018
Published in the United States by DK Publishing
345 Hudson Street, New York, New York 10014

Page design copyright © 2018 Dorling Kindersley Limited
DK, a Division of Penguin Random House LLC

18 19 20 21 22 10 9 8 7 6 5 4 3 2 1
001–305863–April/2018

marvel.com
© 2018 MARVEL

Published in Great Britain by Dorling Kindersley Limited.

A catalog record for this book
is available from the Library of Congress.

ISBN: 978-1-4654-6684-6 (Paperback)
ISBN: 978-1-4654-6685-3 (Hardcover)

DK books are available at special discounts when purchased in bulk for
sales promotions, premiums, fund-raising, or educational use. For details, contact:
DK Publishing Special Markets, 345 Hudson Street, New York, New York 10014
SpecialSales@dk.com

Printed and bound in China

A WORLD OF IDEAS:
SEE ALL THERE IS TO KNOW

www.dk.com

Contents

Fiendish villains

The universe is full of cunning, fearsome Super Villains. These criminals have awesome abilities and use amazing technology.

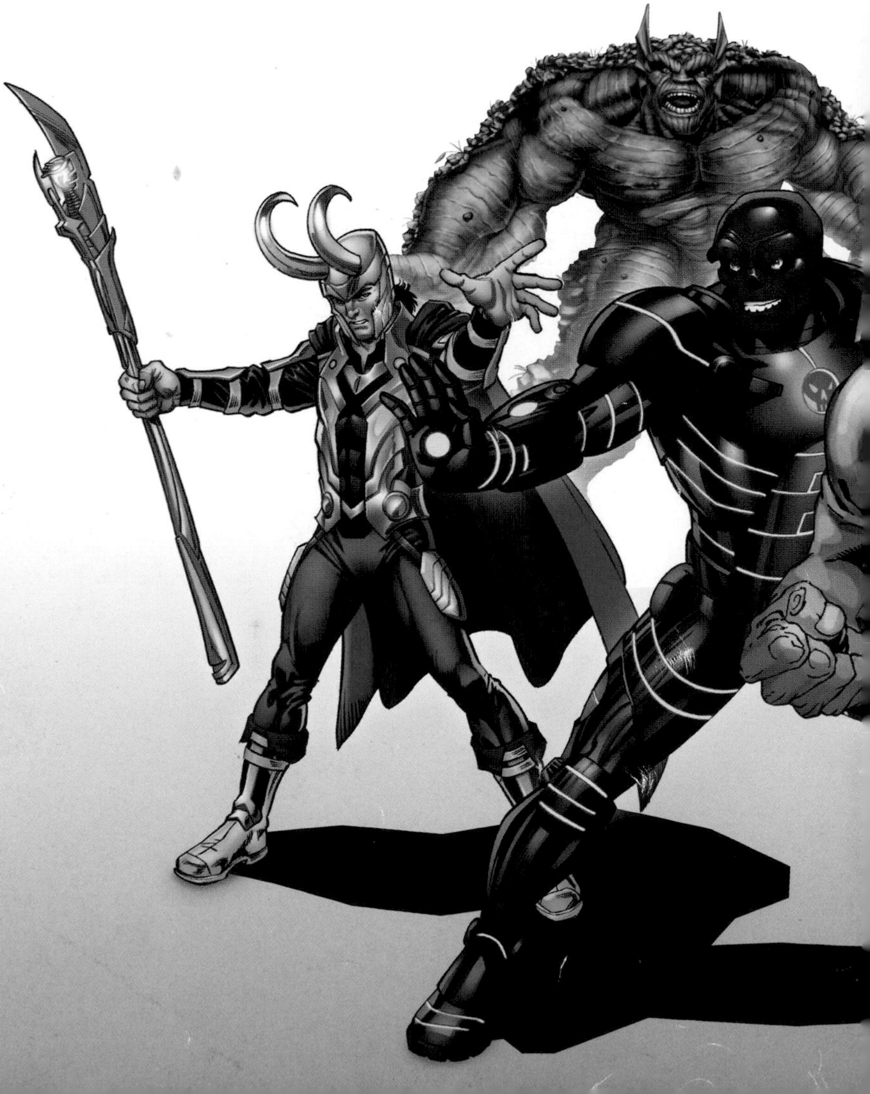

They are always planning evil schemes to get more power. Ultimate villains have Super Hero archenemies, who try to stop them from taking over the world!

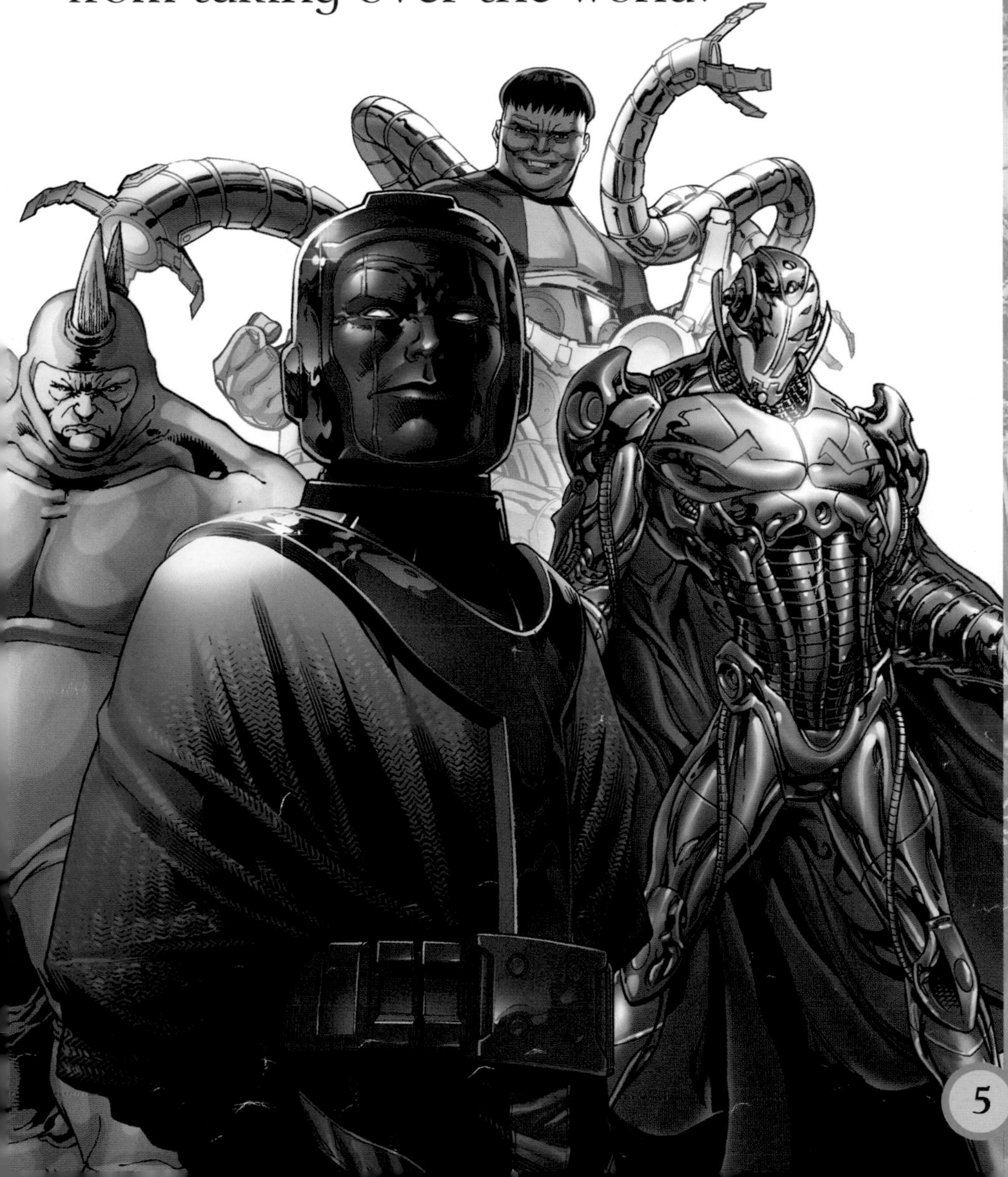

Thanos

Thanos is the ultimate bad guy.

He was born on Saturn's moon, Titan.

Thanos is a sly and cruel villain.

He has a great deal of power,

and is determined to rule the galaxy.

Thanos will destroy anyone

who stands in his way!

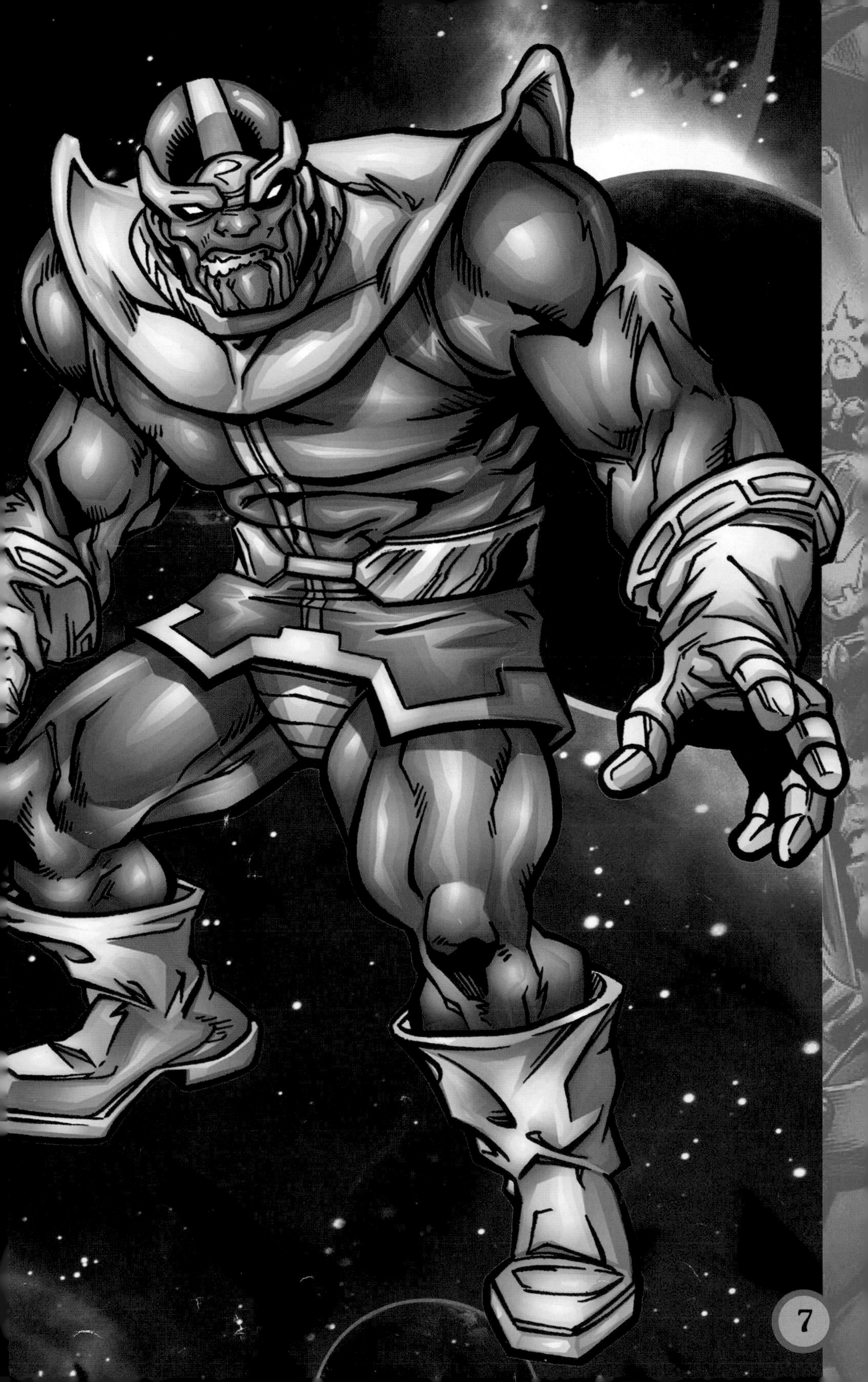

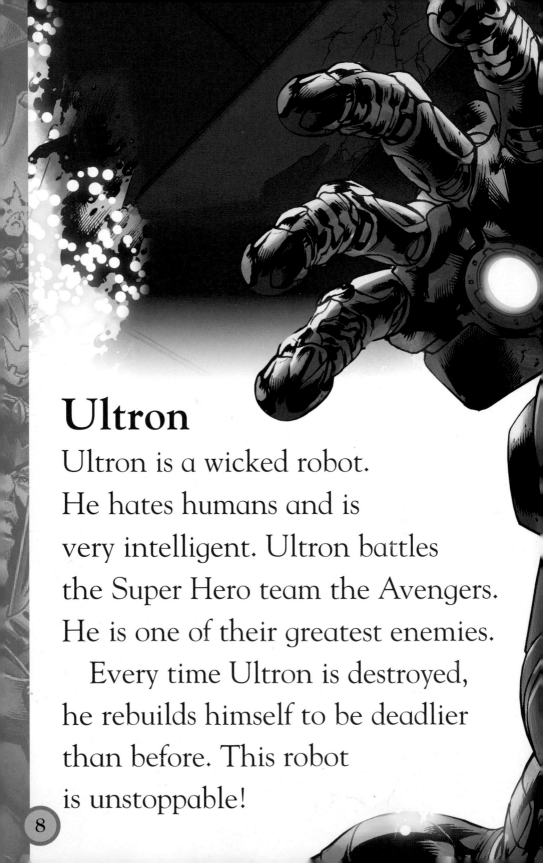

Ultron

Ultron is a wicked robot.
He hates humans and is
very intelligent. Ultron battles
the Super Hero team the Avengers.
He is one of their greatest enemies.

   Every time Ultron is destroyed,
he rebuilds himself to be deadlier
than before. This robot
is unstoppable!

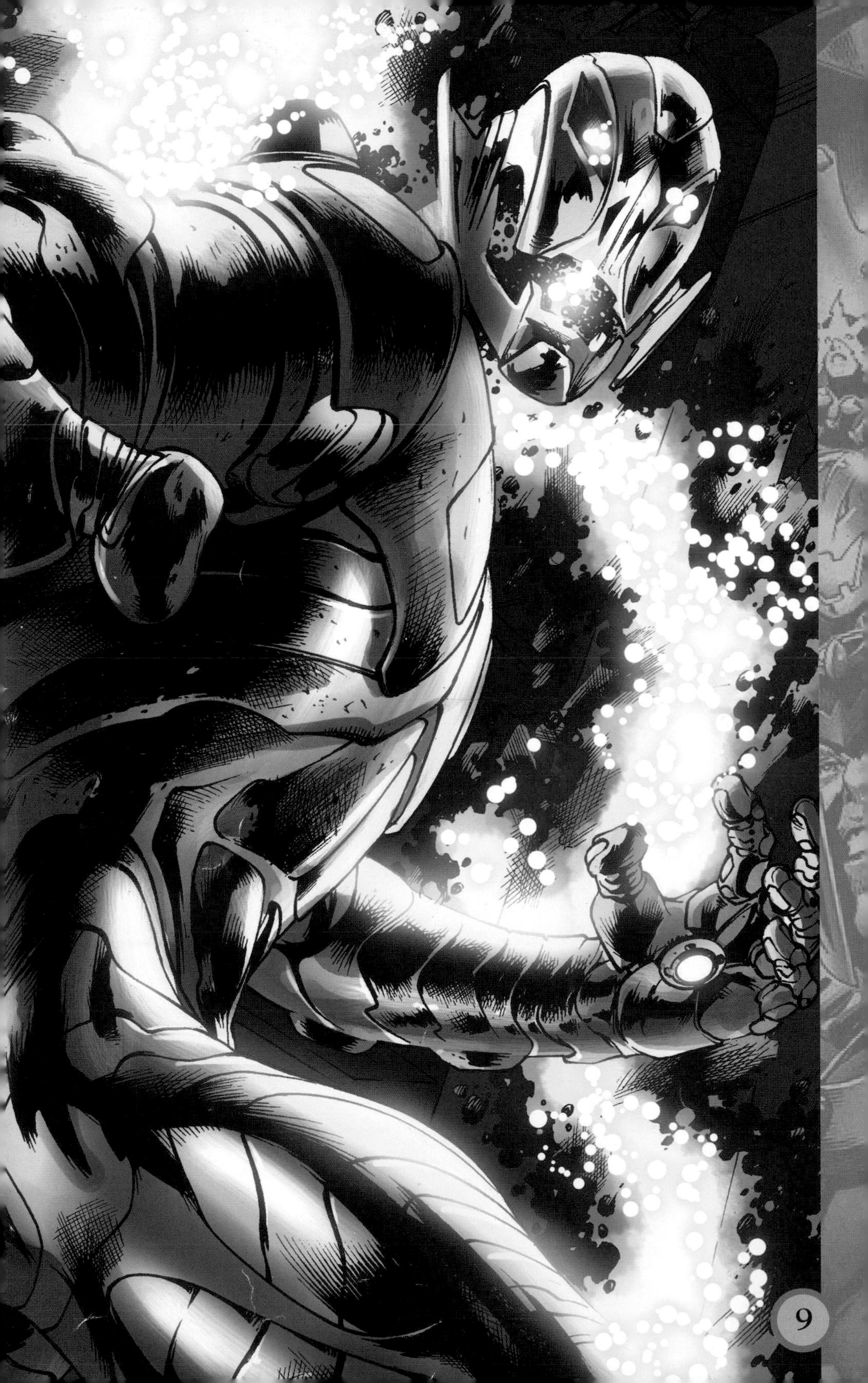

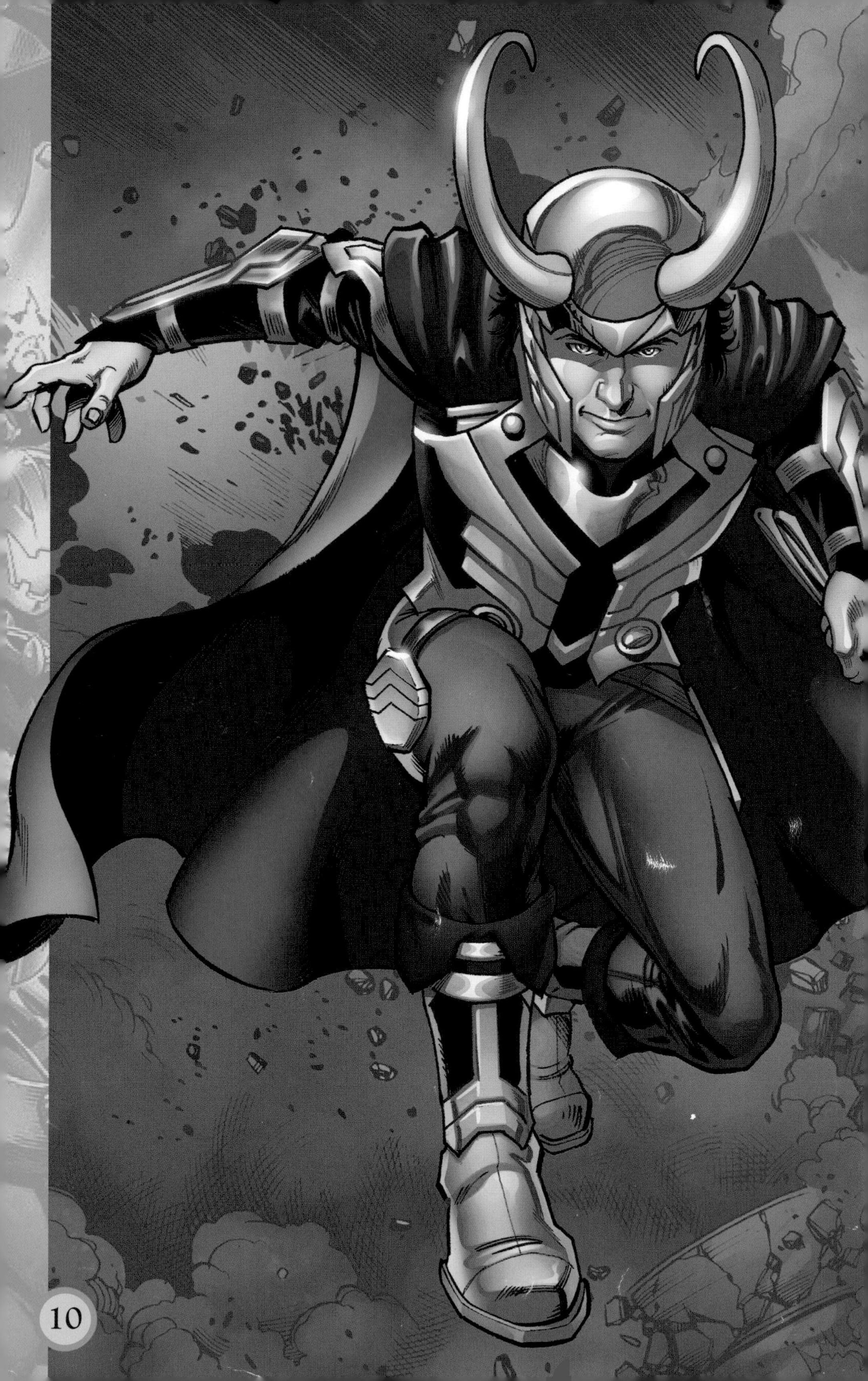

Loki

Loki is the God of Mischief. He is the evil brother of the Thunder God, Thor. He lives in the magical kingdom of Asgard.

Loki can shape-shift into any form he chooses. He uses black magic to play tricks, and to cause mayhem for the Avengers.

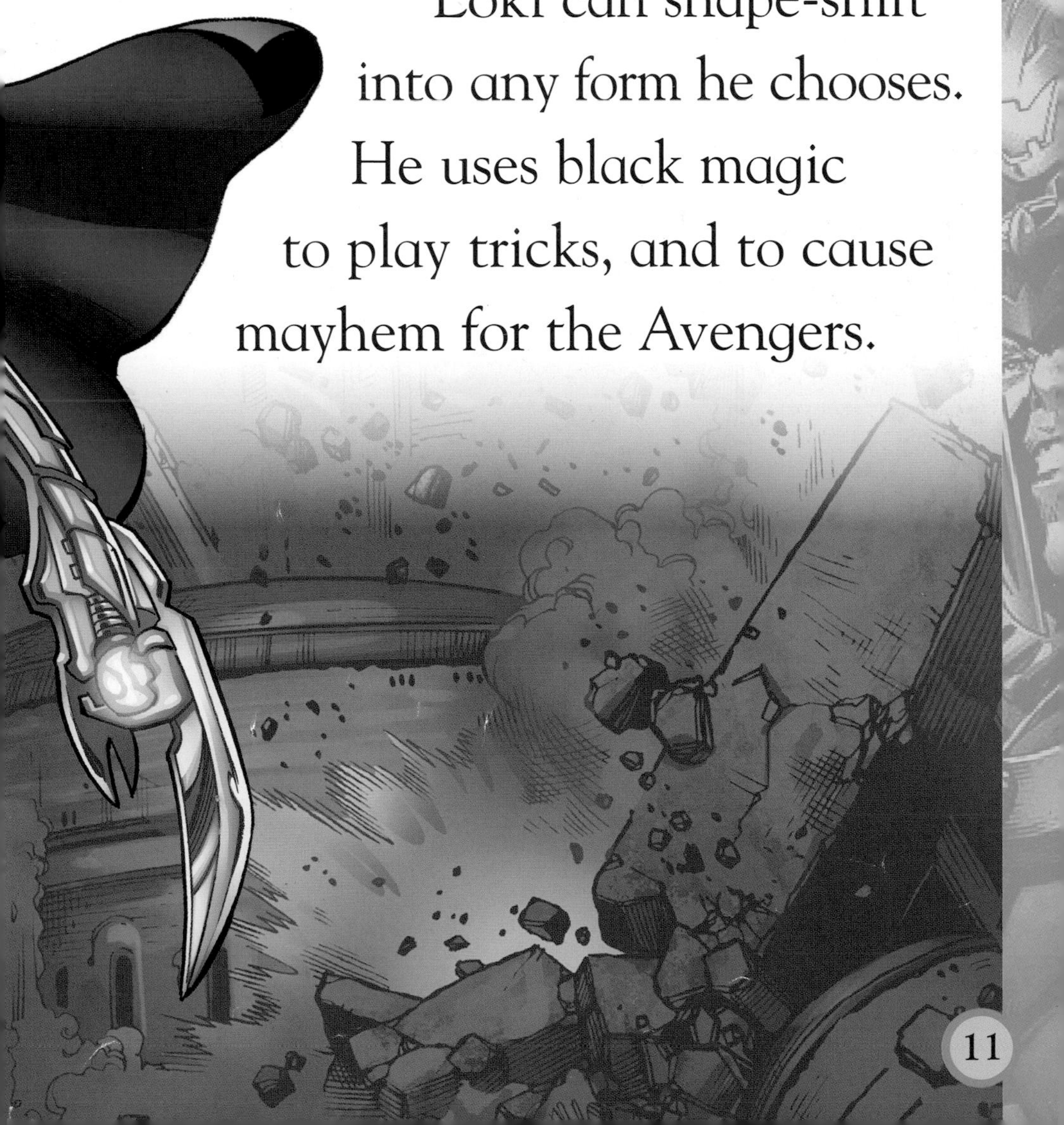

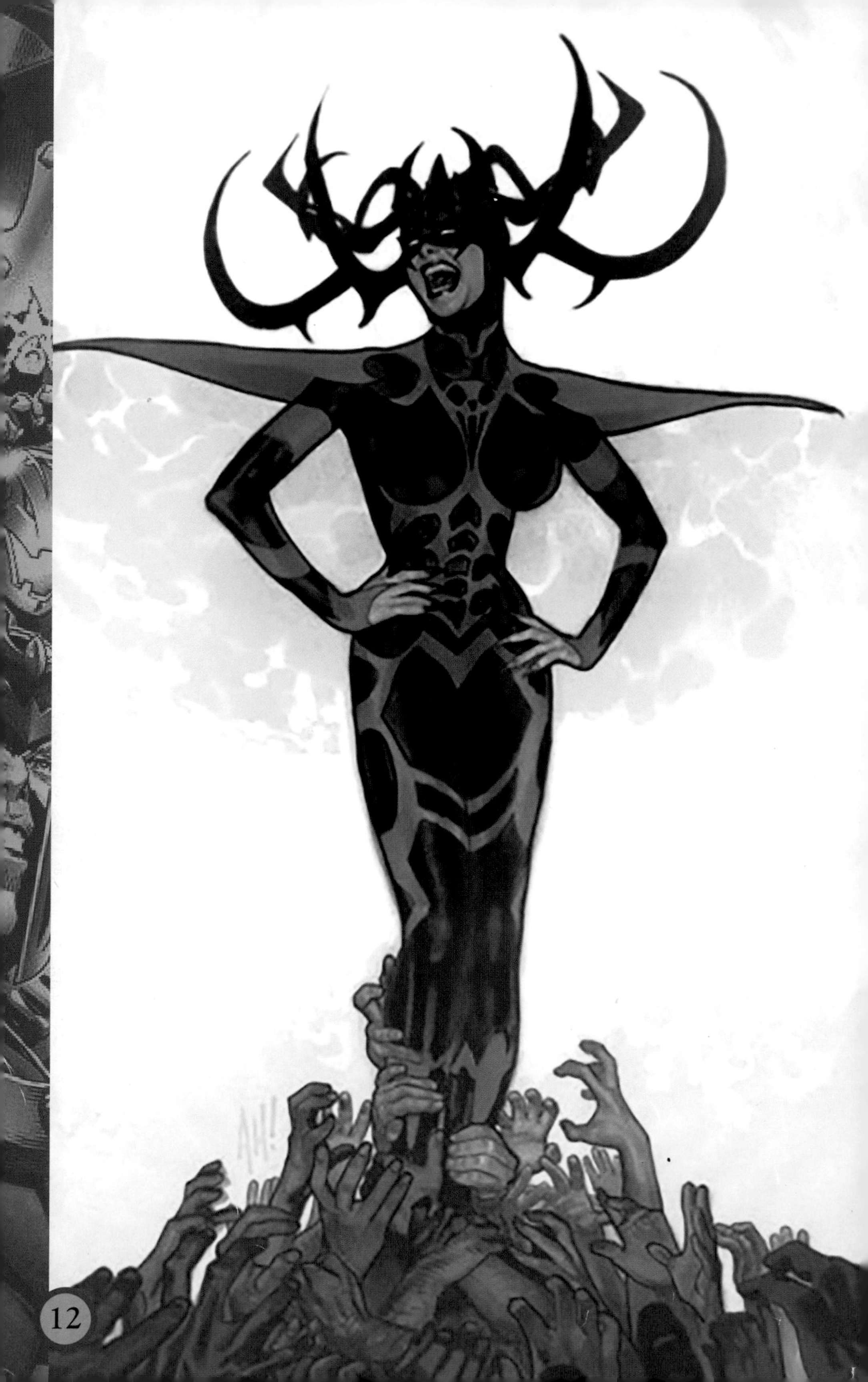
AH!

Hela

Hela is the Goddess of Death. She reigns over Hel, the creepy land of the dead. She wants to trap all gods and mortals in her cruel kingdom forever!

Hela has the power to kill with just one touch. The goddess also has a powerful weapon named Nightsword, but she prefers to use magic.

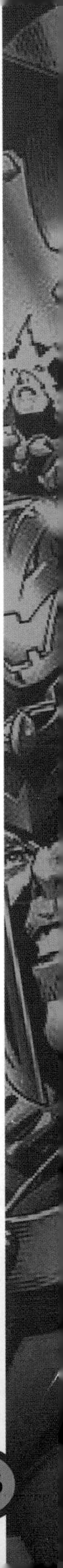

Doctor Octopus

Doctor Octopus has four menacing, mechanical tentacles. They became part of his body after an accident. He can move them using only his mind. His tentacles are super-strong.

Doctor Octopus is a brilliant scientist, but he is also a crook. He is a constant threat to the wall-climbing Super Hero Spider-Man, and to Spidey's family and friends.

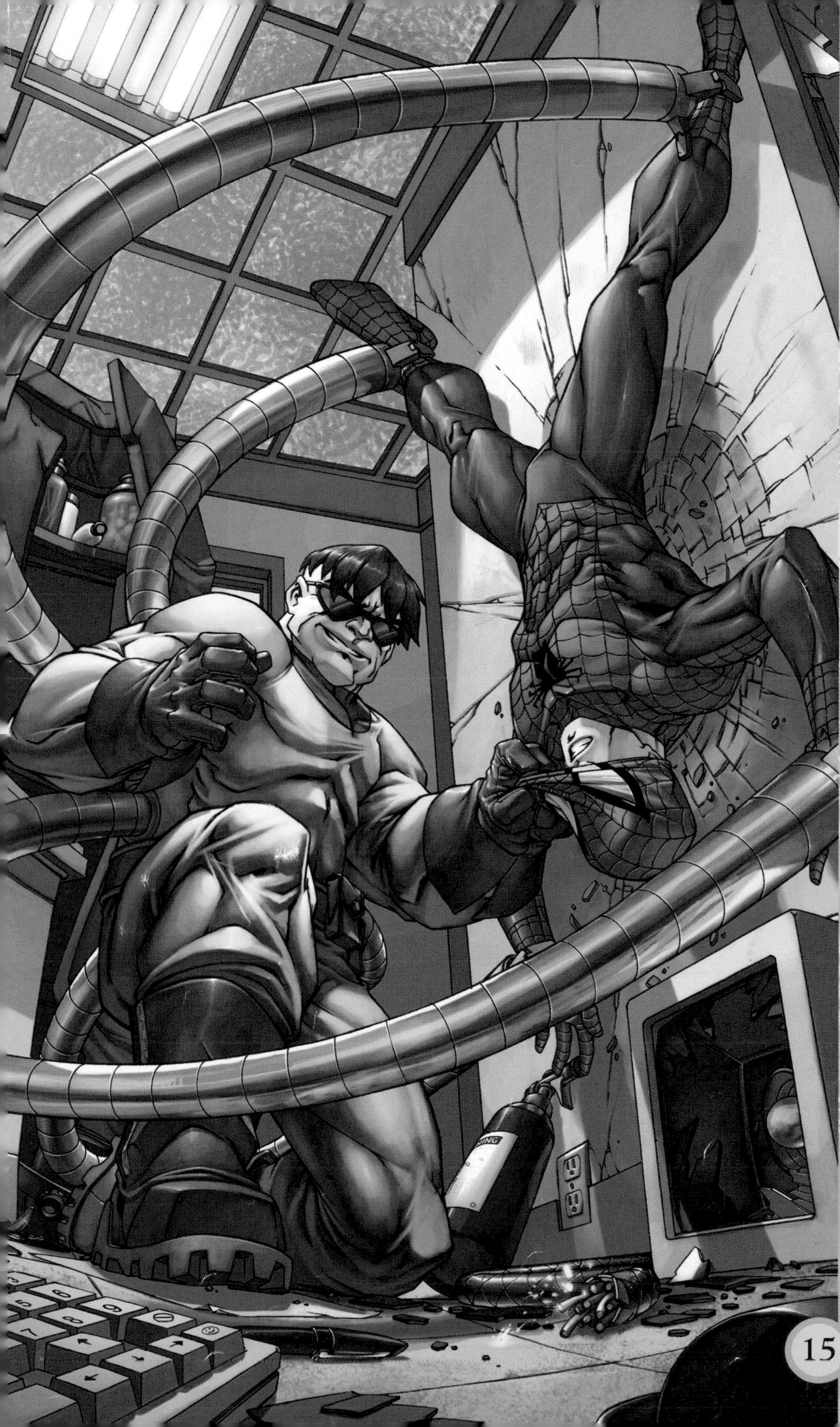

VILLAINOUS TEAMS

It isn't just heroes that form super-teams. Wicked villains join deadly groups, too. These criminals can conquer the universe with powerful allies by their sides!

Hydra

This evil organization of villains causes total chaos. Hydra uses secret agents to fight the Avengers.

Sinister Six

Doctor Octopus set up this mean team to combat Spider-Man. Many members leave and join over time.

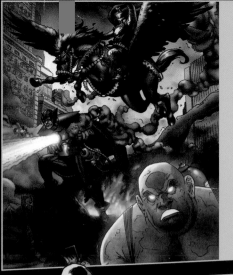

Masters of Evil

This criminal group
was created in order
to battle the Avengers.
The Masters of Evil
have lots of different
powers and weapons.

Serpent Society

Only snake-themed villains
such as Viper and Cobra
can join this evil group.

Circus of Crime

This team hypnotizes
its audiences and
steals from them
during circus shows.
The group fights heroes
such as Hawkeye.

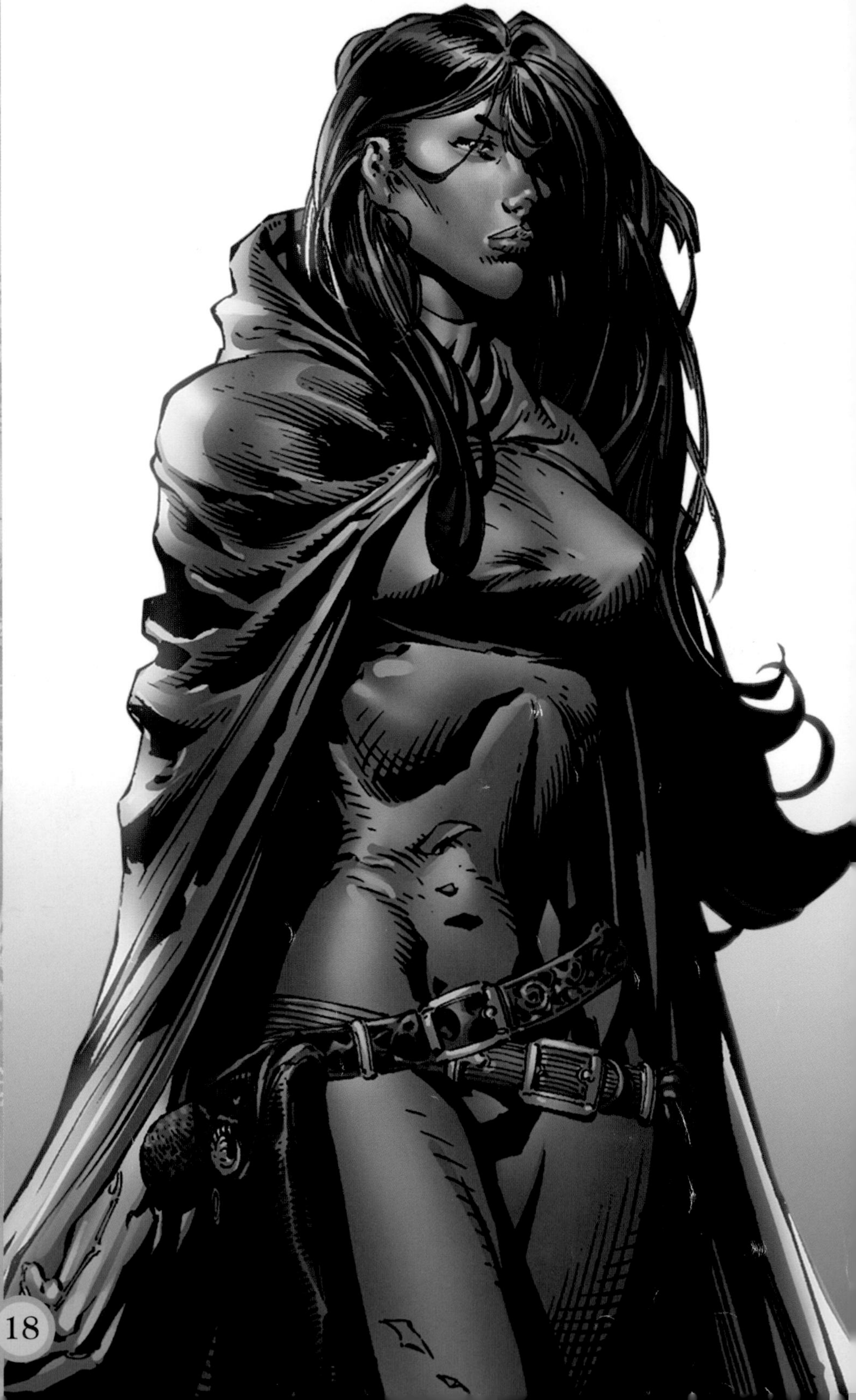

Madame Hydra

Madame Hydra trained as a spy before she became the leader of Hydra. This snake-themed villain is also known as Viper. She is the leader of the sneaky Serpent Society, too.

Madame Hydra's favorite weapon is poison. She uses poison darts, toxic lipstick, and her hollowed fangs to deliver deadly venom.

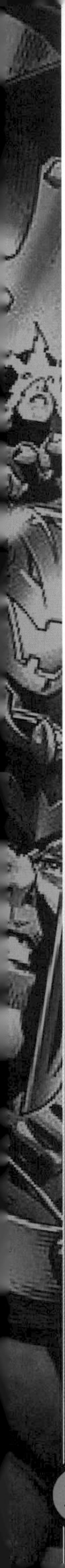

Red Skull

Red Skull is very wicked.
He is so evil that even other
Super Villains do not want
to work with him.

Red Skull is able to transfer
his mind into other people's bodies.
This means he can live forever!
The brave Super Hero
Captain America finds it
difficult to destroy him.

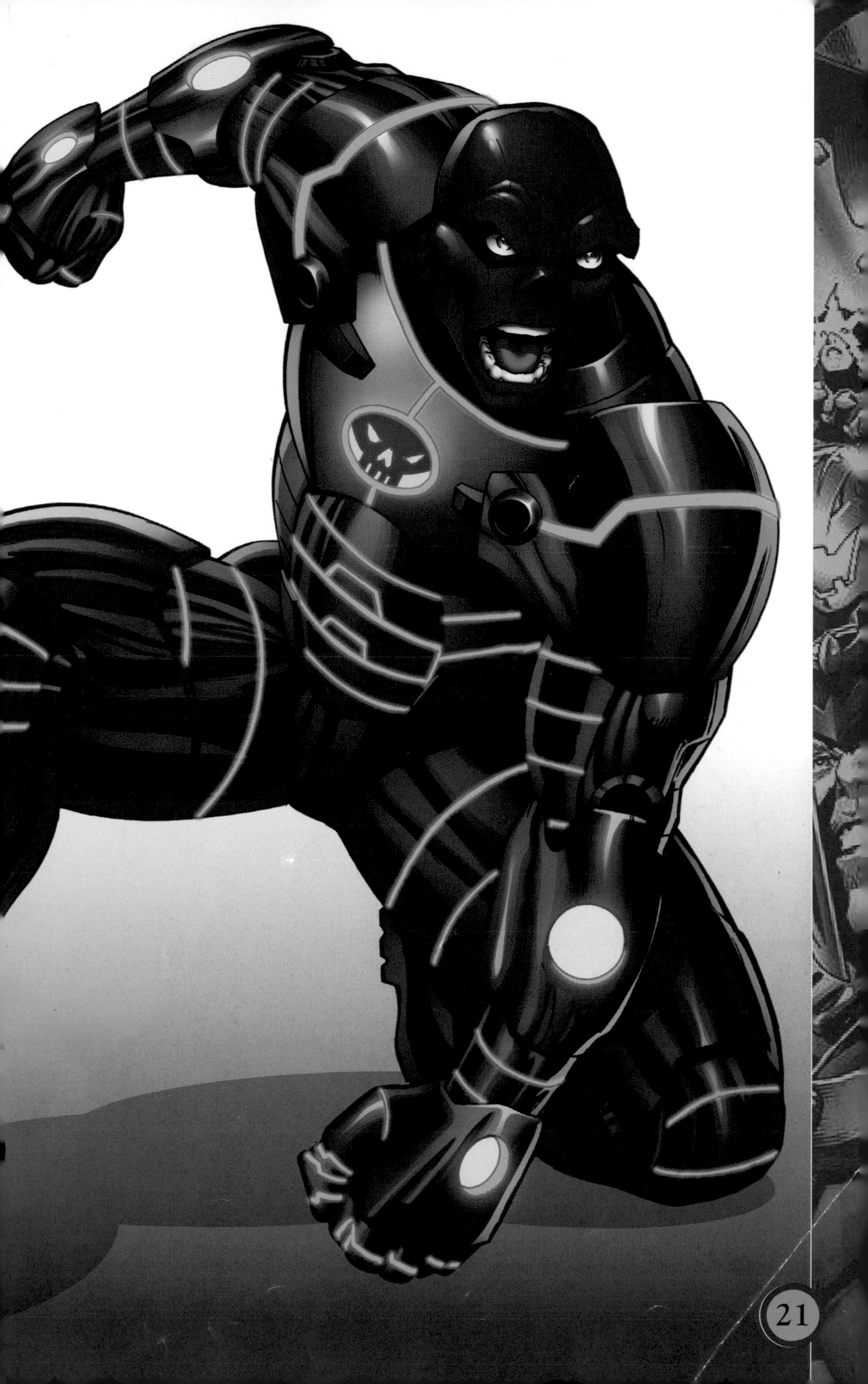

Green Goblin

Norman Osborn is the Green Goblin. He is mean and cunning. This Super Villain flies around New York on his Goblin Glider, causing trouble.

Green Goblin became a crime lord in order to take over the world. He also wants to crush the web-slinging Spider-Man!

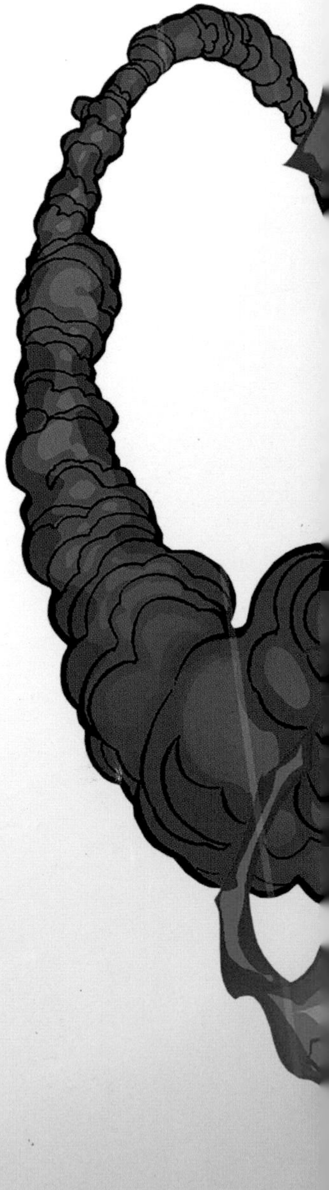

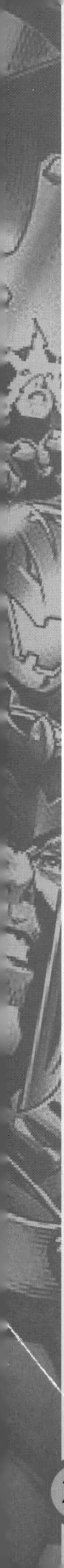

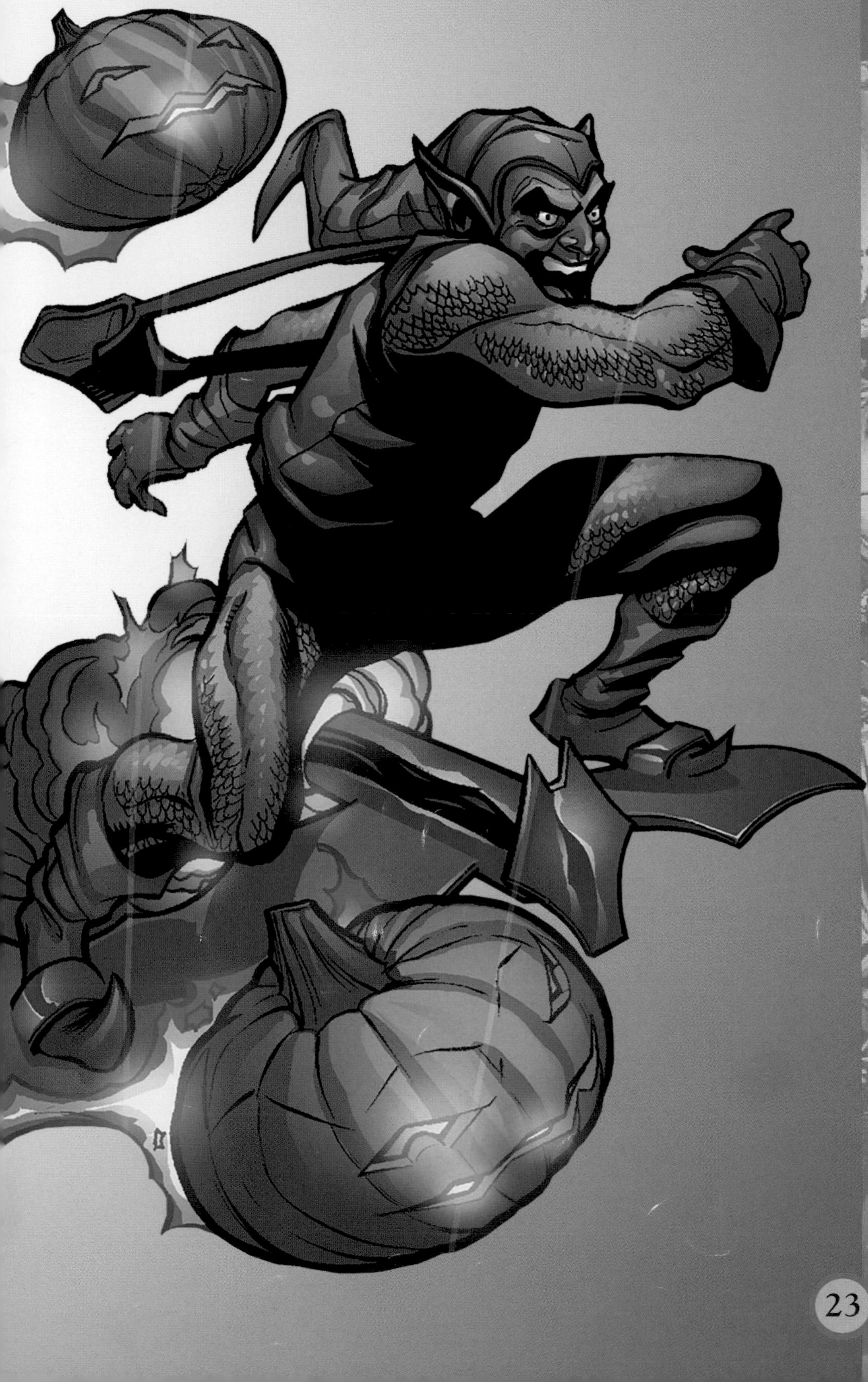

Kang

Kang the Conqueror is a human from the distant future. He uses a time machine to travel through time and space. This villain wants to conquer all the worlds across the universe.

Kang's intelligence, futuristic armor, and hi-tech weapons make him a fearsome foe. Even the Avengers find him hard to beat!

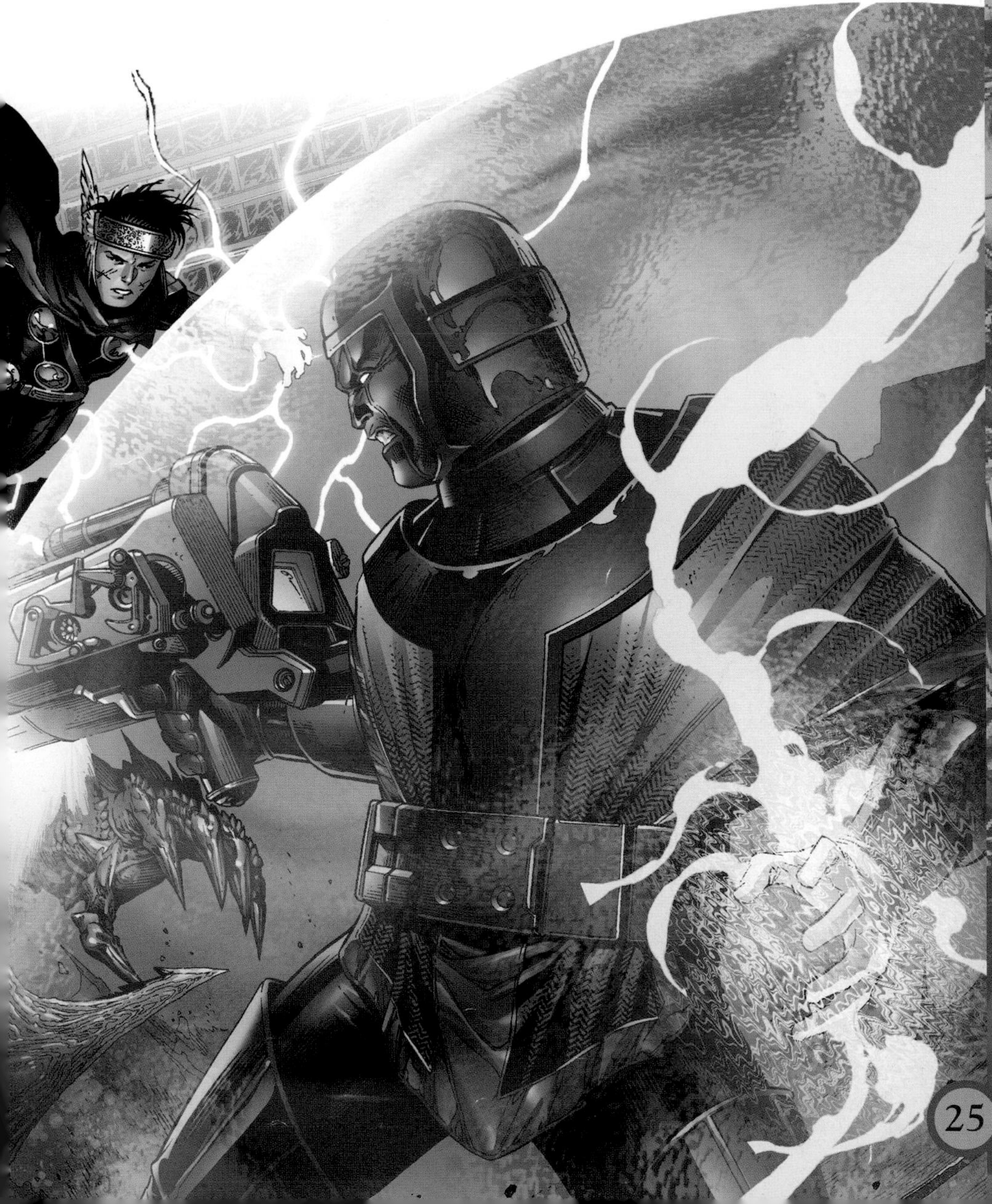

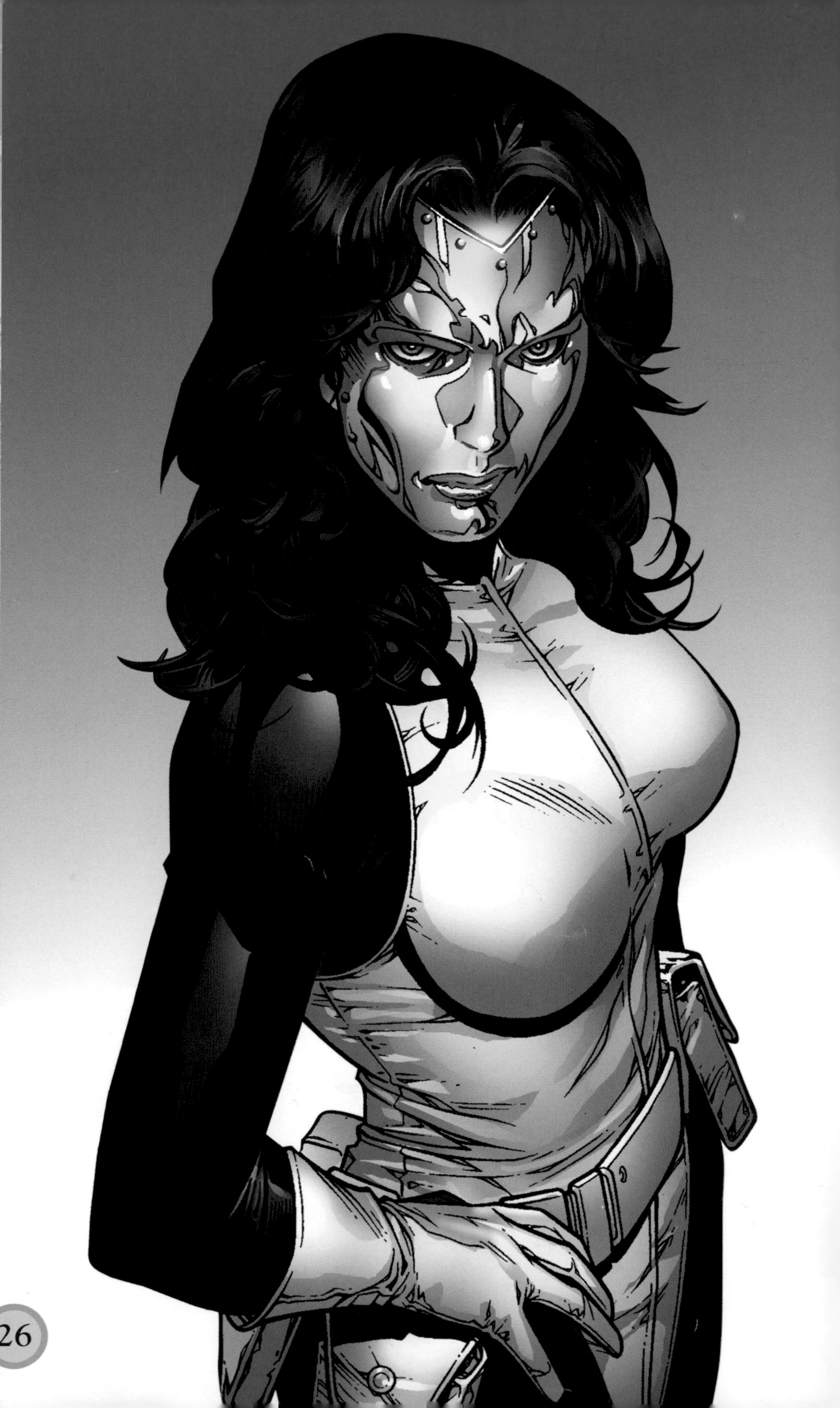

Madame Masque

Madame Masque often fights
the Super Hero Iron Man.
She is the leader of the criminal
group known as the Maggia.

Madame Masque is smart,
sneaky, and deadly. Her gold mask
hides scars that she received in a
terrible accident. She is very good
at disguising herself as other people.

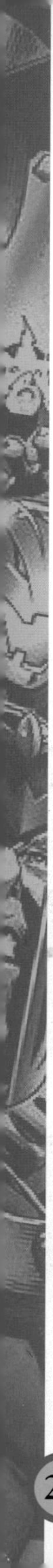

Dormammu

Dormammu is an all-powerful being made of mystic energy. He is the fiery lord of a strange realm known as the Dark Dimension.

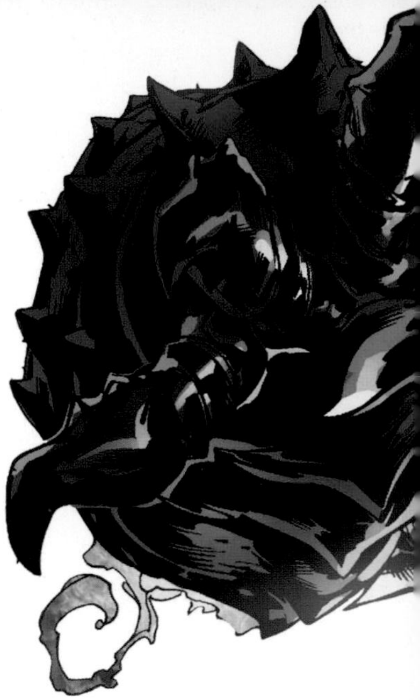

Dormammu seeks to rule all the dimensions in the universe. He is always stopped by Doctor Strange, the strongest sorcerer on Earth.

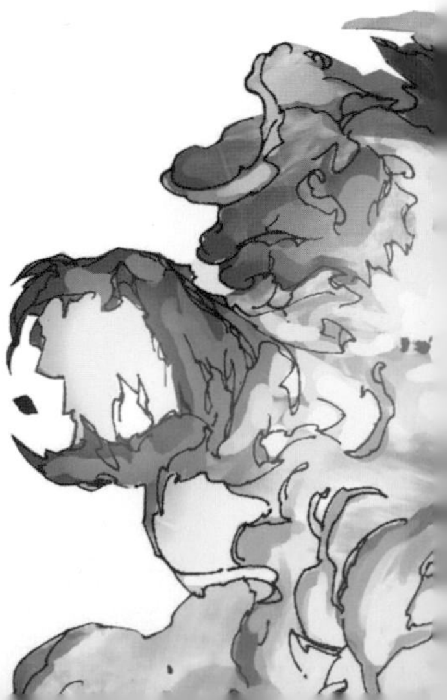

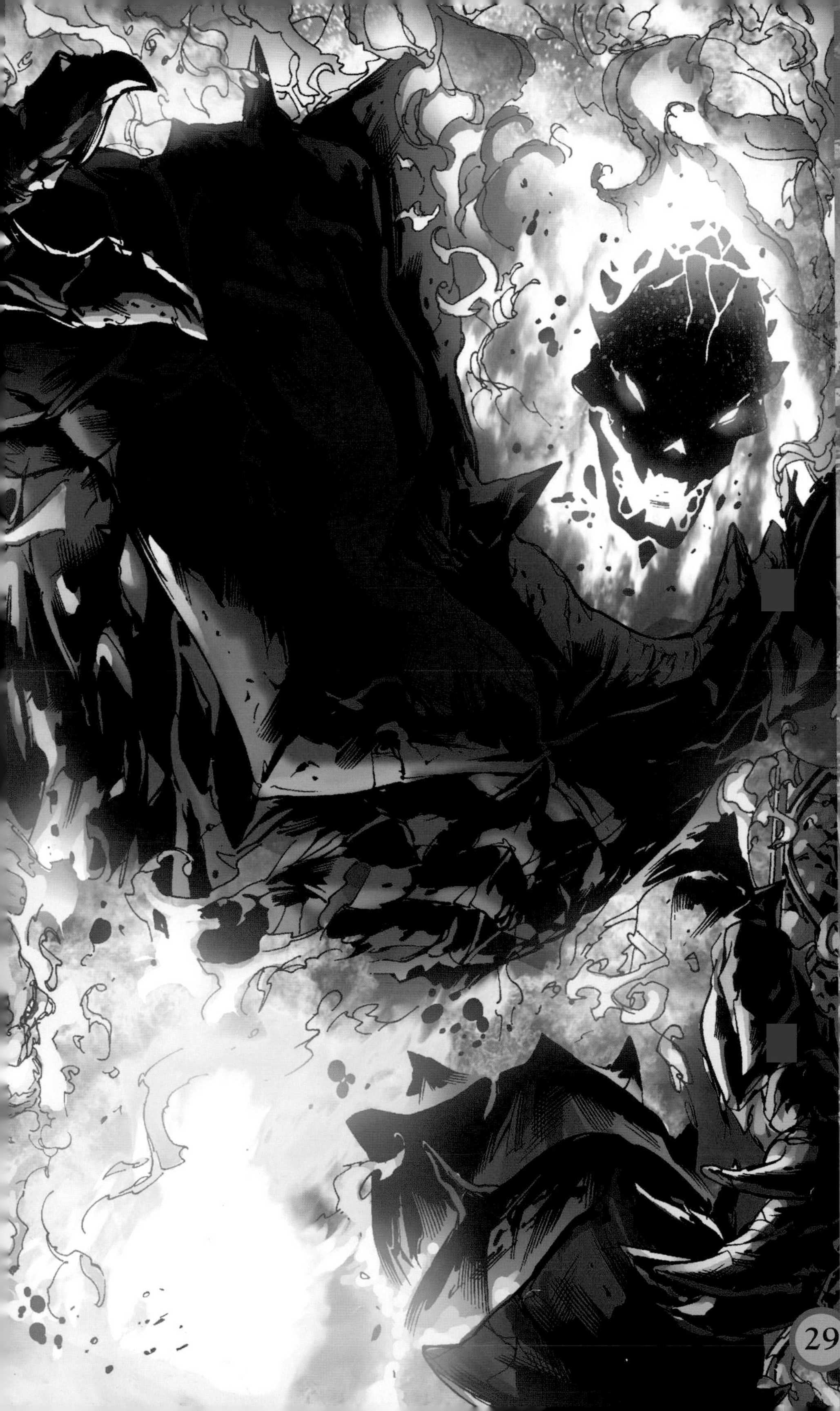

CRIMINAL LOCATIONS

Villains need kingdoms and bases where they can make evil plans. If these crooks are caught by brave heroes, they are locked up in super-secure prisons!

Hel

Hela controls Hel, the land of the dead. She can change the landscape with just her mind.

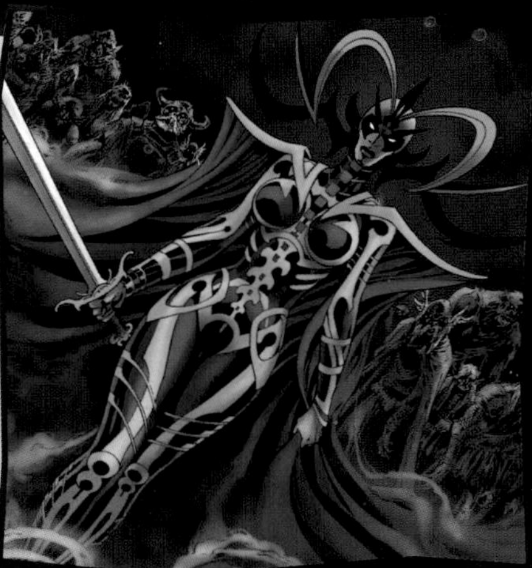

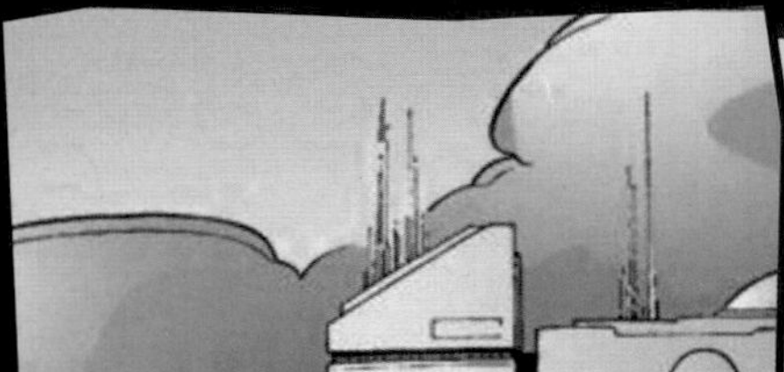

The Big House

This prison is named the Big House, but it is actually tiny! Scientist Hank Pym shrinks criminals down to very small sizes, so they can fit inside.

Oscorp Tower

Oscorp is the Green Goblin's company. The company is based at the Oscorp Tower. All of the villain's technology is made here.

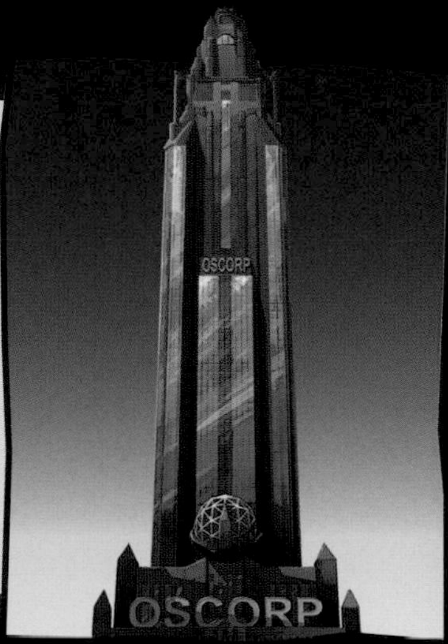
OSCORP
OSCORP

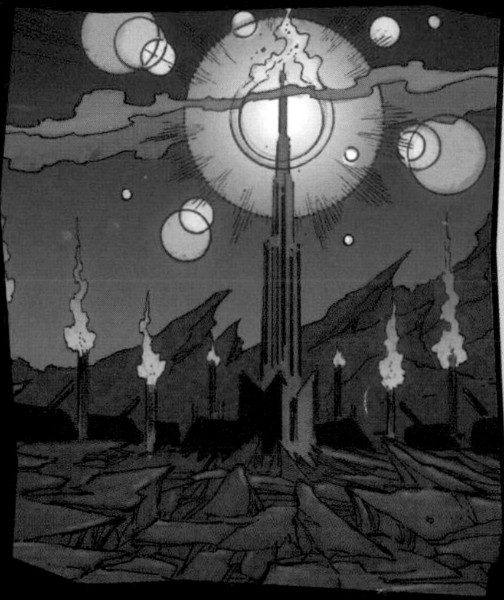

Dark Dimension

This creepy dimension is enormous! The worlds that Dormammu rules are kept here. He adds to his collection all the time.

The Kyln

Criminals beware, the Kyln is a Super Villain prison! These ball-shaped jail cells can be found in outer space.

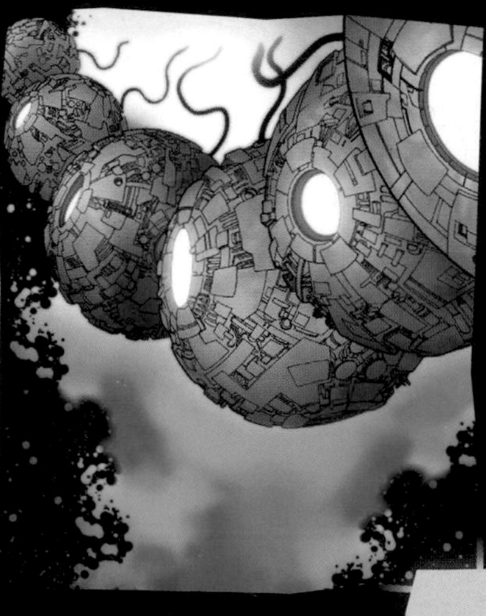

Abomination

This reptile-like monster was once a human. He was transformed into a scaly creature by the same gamma radiation that created the Super Hero Hulk.

Abomination is as mean as he is ugly. This villain wants to prove he is stronger than Hulk, but he never succeeds.

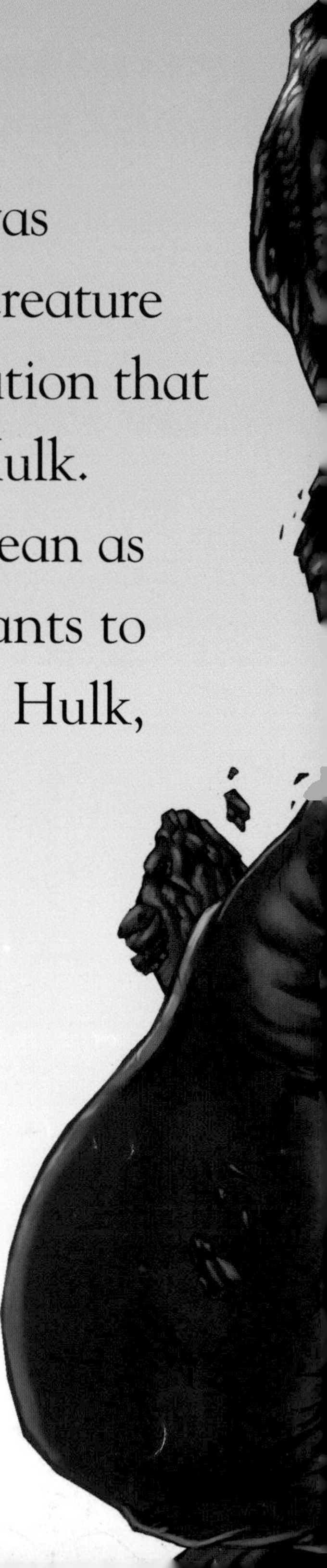

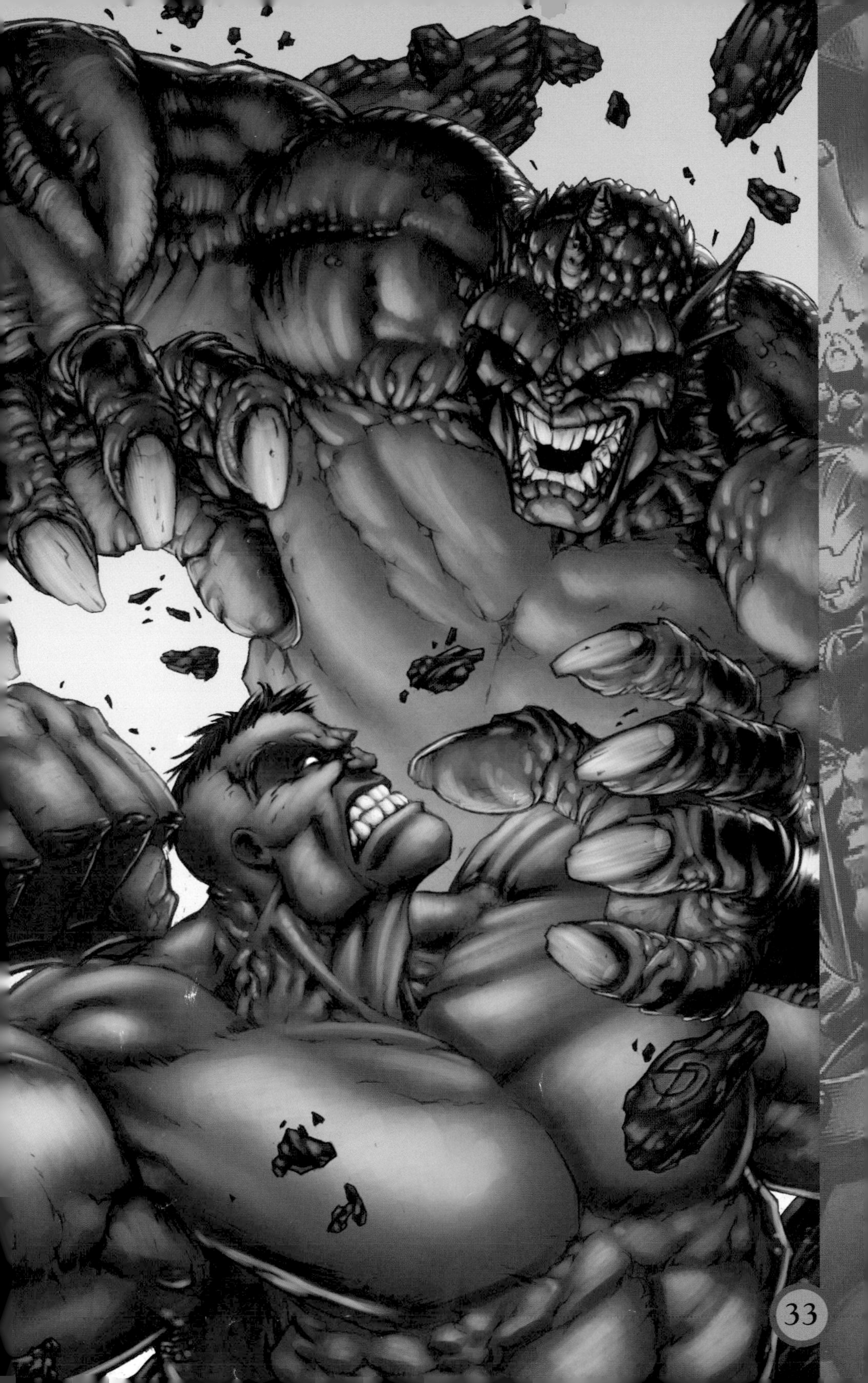

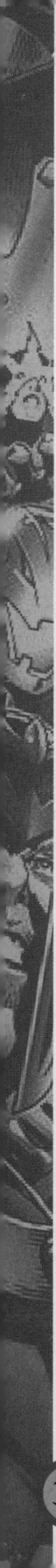

M.O.D.O.K.

M.O.D.O.K. is a mad scientist who wants to rule the world. He is part-man, part-computer. This odd-looking Super Villain uses a hover-chair to move, because his huge head makes walking very difficult.

M.O.D.O.K. is always scheming against Super Heroes like Captain America and Hulk. Fortunately, he always loses!

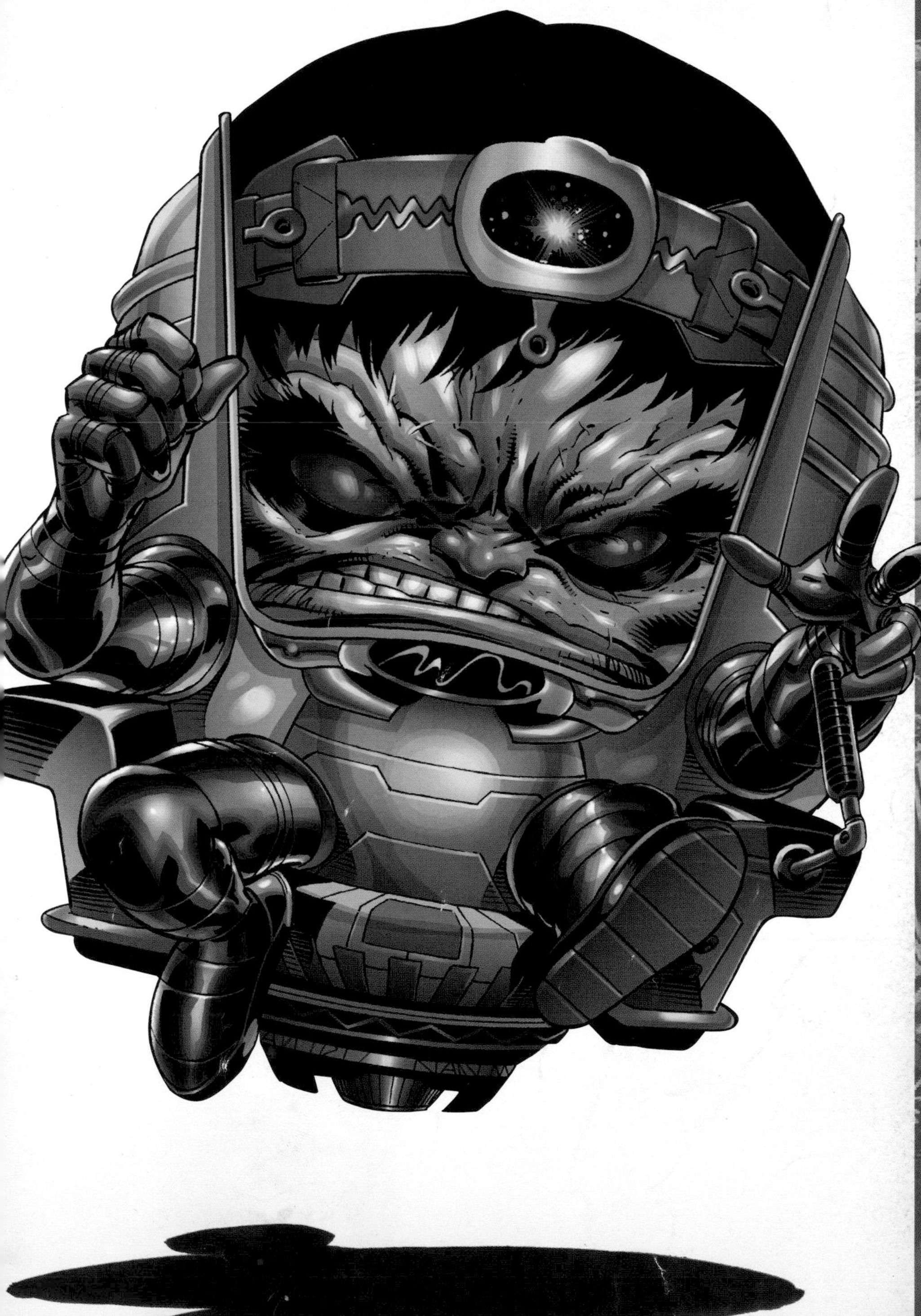

Enchantress

Enchantress is a wicked and powerful goddess from Asgard. She has great magical skills and superhuman strength.

Enchantress longs to rule over the kingdom of Asgard with the Avenger Thor by her side. She tries to use magic to win him over, but he is able to resist her spells.

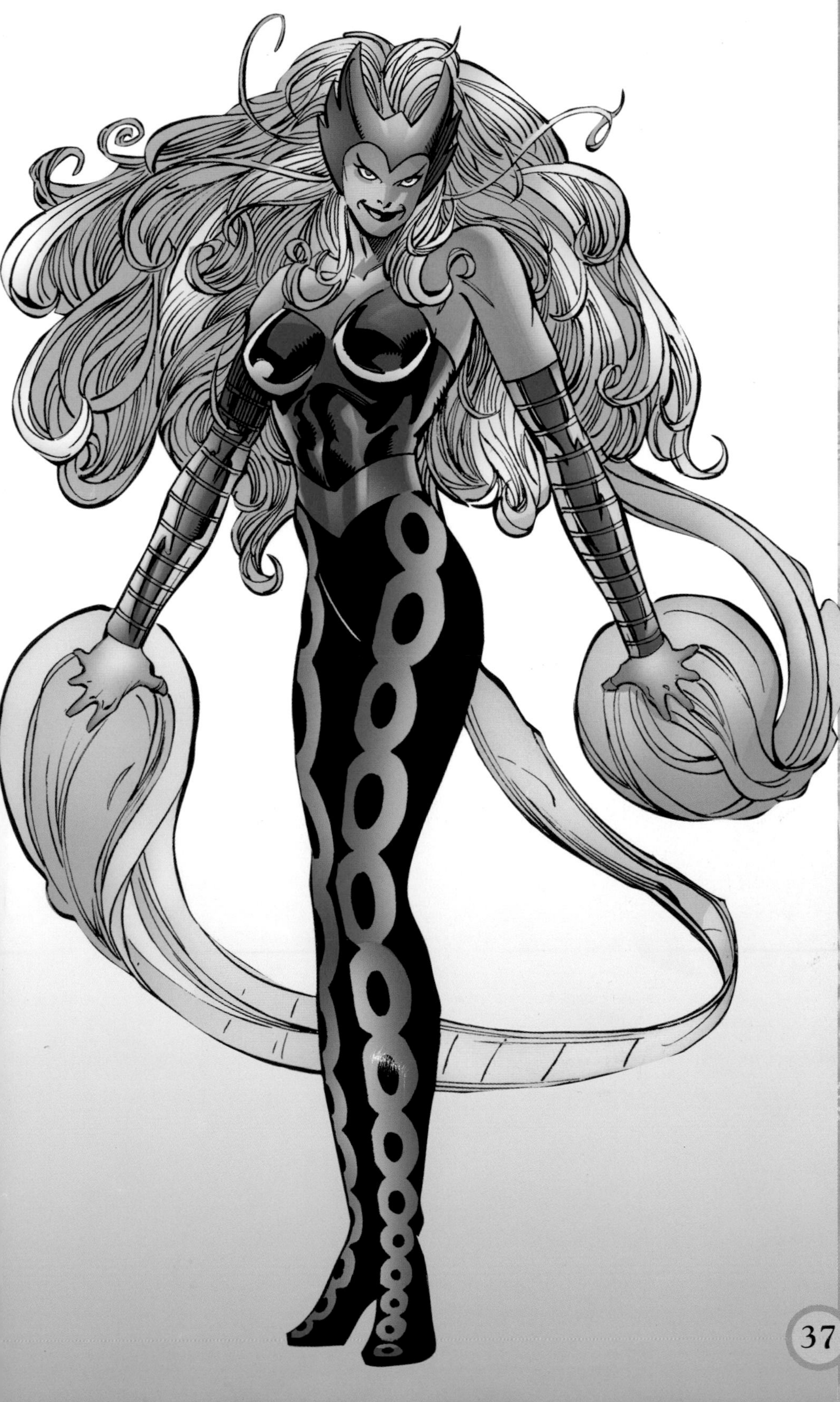

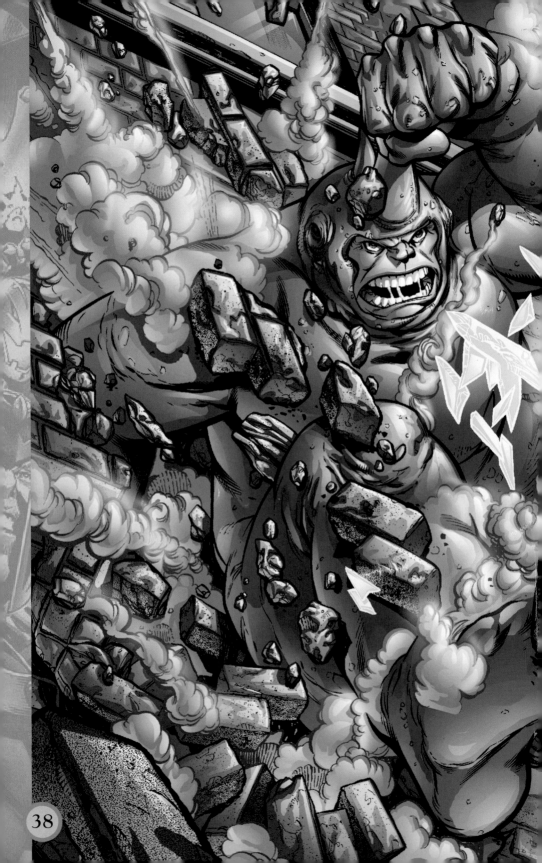

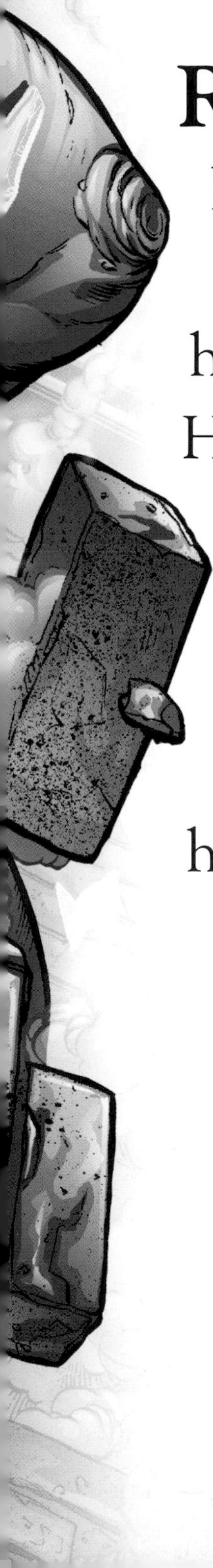

Rhino

Rhino is a superhuman villain. A pair of scientists created him during an experiment. He has rhinoceros-like skin and steel-piercing horns.

Rhino is a fierce fighter, and often battles Spider-Man and Hulk. Fortunately for the heroes, he is not very smart.

Ulysses Klaw

This Super Villain is made of sonic energy. Klaw replaces one of his hands for a powerful sonic blaster.

Klaw was once an assassin. He killed T'Chaka, the King of Wakanda. T'Chaka was also a Super Hero, named Black Panther. T'Chaka's son, T'Challa, became the new Black Panther. Now T'Challa hunts Klaw for revenge.

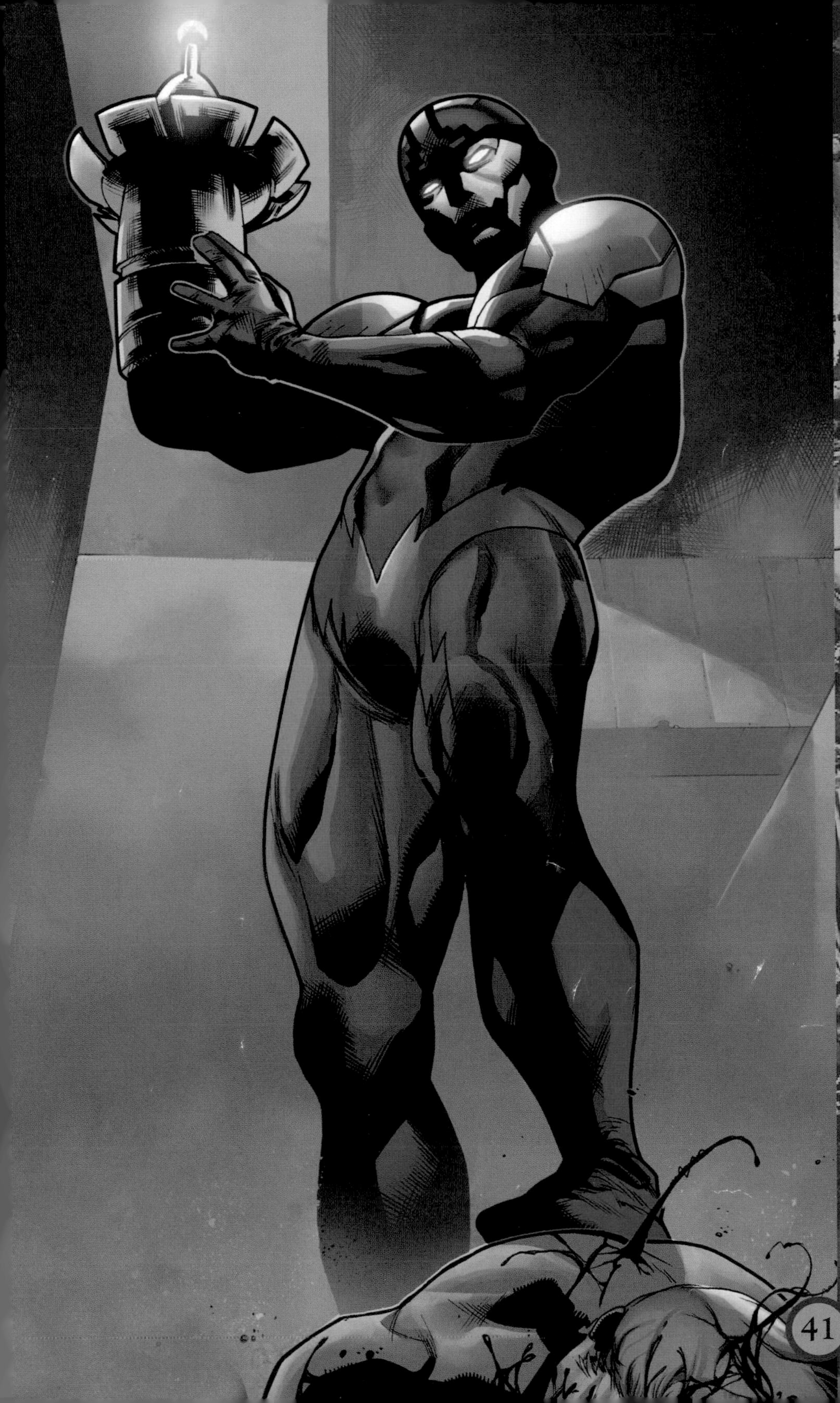

AWESOME OBJECTS

There are many strange and powerful items to help villains defeat annoying heroes.
With magic, or other forces, these devices could destroy the world!

The *Darkhold*

This mysterious book contains many horrible spells. Inside, there are spells for unleashing werewolves and vampires.

Cosmic Cube

The owner of a Cosmic Cube has the power to change reality. It is hard to make a cube, but Red Skull succeeds.

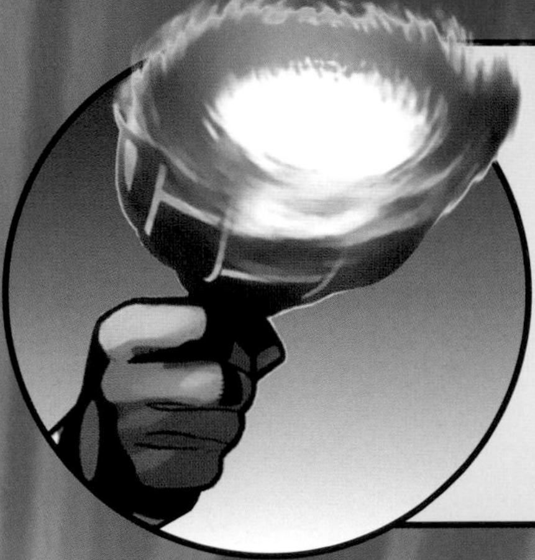

Evil Eye of Avalon

Dormammu uses the Evil Eye to bring Earth into his Dark Dimension. Doctor Strange manages to defeat its power.

Infinity Gauntlet

Thanos uses the Infinity Gauntlet to harness the powers of the six Infinity Gems. The Gems can control everything in the universe!

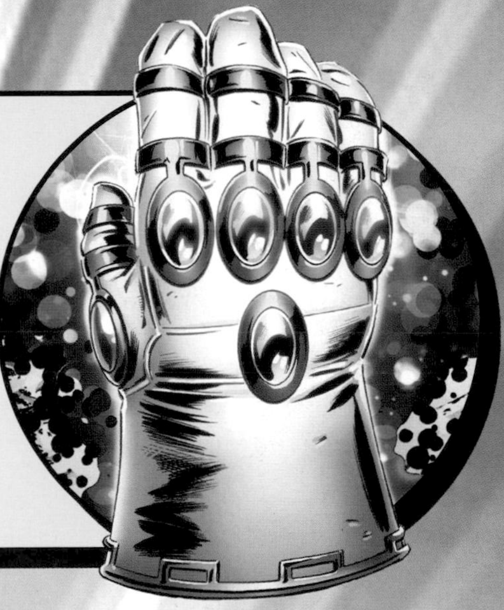

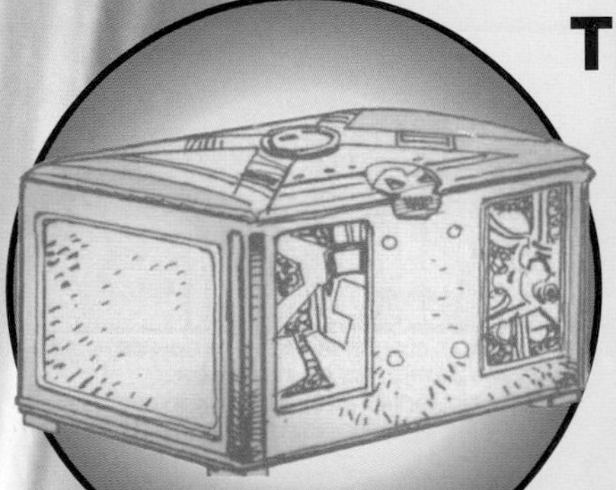

The Casket of Ancient Winters

If this box is opened, a freezing winter will spread across Earth. The trickster Loki uses it in his evil plans.

Quiz

1. Where was Thanos born?

2. Who is the Goddess of Death?

3. What is Madame Hydra's favorite weapon?

4. What does the Green Goblin use to fly around New York?

5. Who lives in the Dark Dimension?

6. What was Abomination before he became a reptile-like monster?

7. Who uses a hover-chair to move around?

8. Who does Enchantress want to rule Asgard with?

9. What did Klaw used to be?

10. Who uses the Infinity Gauntlet?

Answers on page 47

Glossary

archenemies
The main enemies
of someone.

determined
Completely decided
on something.

dimensions
Other worlds that
are not part of ours.

experiment
A test, often carried
out by scientists.

fiendish
Very cruel or unpleasant.

futuristic
From the future.

gamma radiation
A type of dangerous
energy that can change
living things.

hypnotizes
Puts someone in
a sleep-like state.

mechanical
Relating to machines.

menacing
Threatening
or dangerous.

mysterious
Difficult to understand
or explain.

sonic
Relating to sound.

sorcerer
A person with
magical powers.

tentacle
A long, thin arm,
used for holding
things and moving.

transfer
To move from one
place to another.

universe
The whole of space and
everything in it, including
planets, stars, and galaxies.

Index

Answers to the quiz on pages 44 and 45:
1. Saturn's moon, Titan 2. Hela 3. Poison
4. His Goblin Glider 5. Dormammu 6. A human
7. M.O.D.O.K. 8. Thor 9. An assassin 10. Thanos

A LEVEL FOR EVERY READER

This book is a part of an exciting four-level reading series to support children in developing the habit of reading widely for both pleasure and information. Each book is designed to develop a child's reading skills, fluency, grammar awareness, and comprehension in order to build confidence and enjoyment when reading.

Ready for a Level 2 (Beginning to Read) book

A child should:

- be able to recognize a bank of common words quickly and be able to blend sounds together to make some words.
- be familiar with using beginner letter sounds and context clues to figure out unfamiliar words.
- sometimes correct his/her reading if it doesn't look right or make sense.
- be aware of the need for a slight pause at commas and a longer one at periods.

A valuable and shared reading experience

For many children, reading requires much effort, but adult participation can make reading both fun and easier. Here are a few tips on how to use this book with a young reader:

Check out the contents together:

- read about the book on the back cover and talk about the contents page to help heighten interest and expectation.
- discuss new or difficult words.
- chat about labels, annotations, and pictures.

Support the reader:

- give the book to the young reader to turn the pages.
- where necessary, encourage longer words to be broken into syllables, sound out each one, and then flow the syllables together; ask him/her to reread the sentence to check the meaning.
- encourage the reader to vary her/his voice as she/he reads; demonstrate how to do this if helpful.

Talk at the end of each book, or after every few pages:

- ask questions about the text and the meaning of the words used—this helps develop comprehension skills.
- read the quiz at the end of the book and encourage the reader to answer the questions, if necessary, by turning back to the relevant pages to find the answers.

Series consultant, Dr. Linda Gambrell, Distinguished Professor of Education at Clemson University, has served as President of the National Reading Conference, the College Reading Association, and the International Reading Association.